D1605427

You made the best decision by choosing us,

congratulations!

The next page will be about your special reward to thank you for choosing our book.

SPECIAL BONUS!

Want this bonus book for FREE?

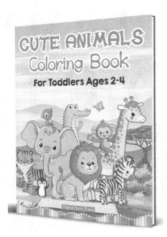

Scan The QR Code To Get Your Free Book!

MERRY CHRISTMAS

THIS BOOK BELONGS TO:

YOU CAN COLOR THE ILLUSTRATIONS IN EACH PAGE FOR EXTRA FUN!

ALPHABET

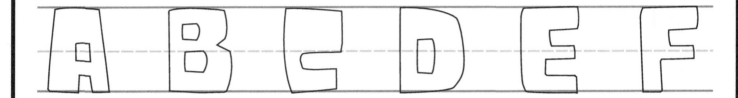

A B C D E F

G H I J K L

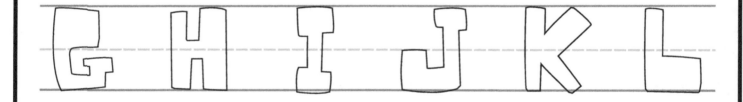

M N O P Q R

I SPY WITH MY LITTLE EYE SOMETHING STARTING WITH

IS FOR

Angel

I SPY WITH MY LITTLE EYE
SOMETHING STARTING WITH

IS FOR

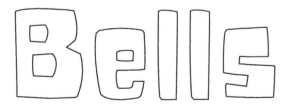

I SPY WITH MY LITTLE EYE SOMETHING STARTING WITH

IS FOR

CandyCane

I SPY WITH MY LITTLE EYE SOMETHING STARTING WITH

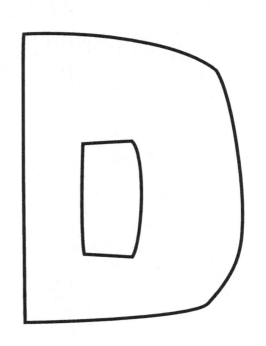

IS FOR

I SPY WITH MY LITTLE EYE SOMETHING STARTING WITH

IS FOR

I SPY WITH MY LITTLE EYE SOMETHING STARTING WITH

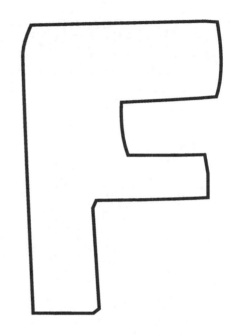

IS FOR

Fruit Cake

I SPY WITH MY LITTLE EYE SOMETHING STARTING WITH

IS FOR

Gingerbread

I SPY WITH MY LITTLE EYE SOMETHING STARTING WITH

IS FOR

Holly

I SPY WITH MY LITTLE EYE
SOMETHING STARTING WITH

IS FOR

Ice skate

I SPY WITH MY LITTLE EYE
SOMETHING STARTING WITH

IS FOR

Jingle Bells

I SPY WITH MY LITTLE EYE SOMETHING STARTING WITH

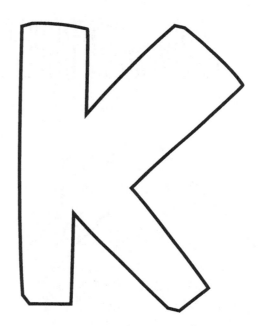

IS FOR

King

I SPY WITH MY LITTLE EYE SOMETHING STARTING WITH

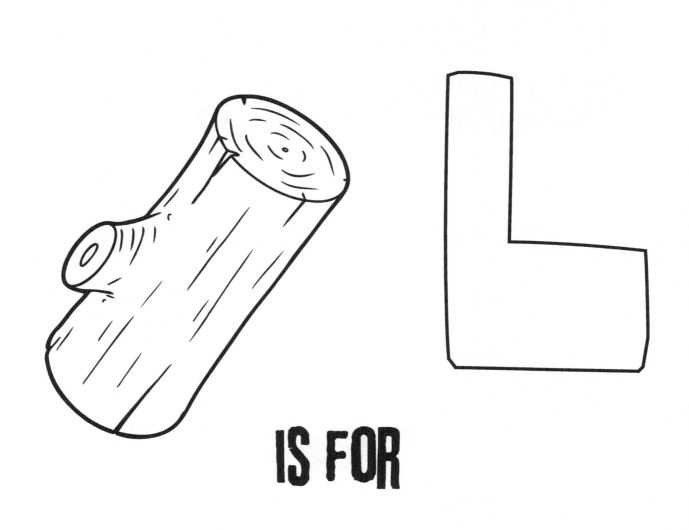

IS FOR

I SPY WITH MY LITTLE EYE SOMETHING STARTING WITH

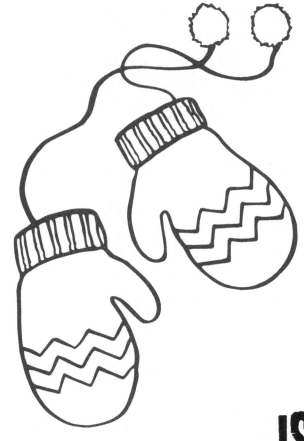

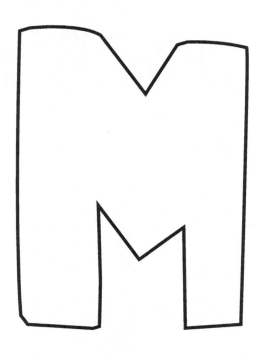

IS FOR

Mitten

I SPY WITH MY LITTLE EYE SOMETHING STARTING WITH

 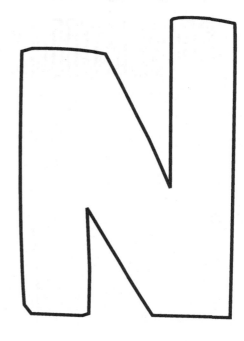

IS FOR

Nutmeg

I SPY WITH MY LITTLE EYE
SOMETHING STARTING WITH

IS FOR

Ornaments

I SPY WITH MY LITTLE EYE SOMETHING STARTING WITH

IS FOR

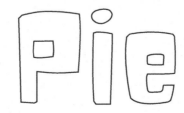

I SPY WITH MY LITTLE EYE SOMETHING STARTING WITH

IS FOR

Quince

I SPY WITH MY LITTLE EYE SOMETHING STARTING WITH

IS FOR

Reindeer

I SPY WITH MY LITTLE EYE SOMETHING STARTING WITH

S

IS FOR

Snowman

I SPY WITH MY LITTLE EYE SOMETHING STARTING WITH

IS FOR

Teddy Bear

I SPY WITH MY LITTLE EYE
SOMETHING STARTING WITH

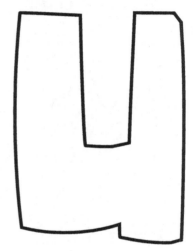

IS FOR

Uniform

I SPY WITH MY LITTLE EYE SOMETHING STARTING WITH

IS FOR

Vixen

I SPY WITH MY LITTLE EYE SOMETHING STARTING WITH

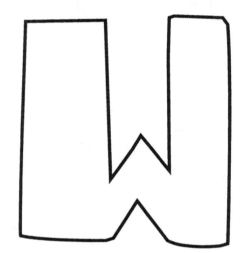

IS FOR

Wreath

I SPY WITH MY LITTLE EYE SOMETHING STARTING WITH

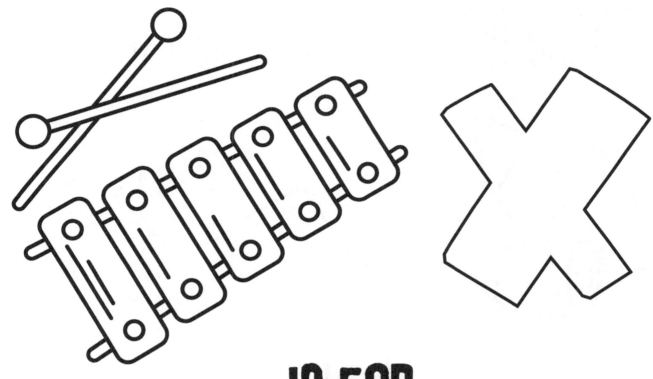

IS FOR

Xylophone

I SPY WITH MY LITTLE EYE
SOMETHING STARTING WITH

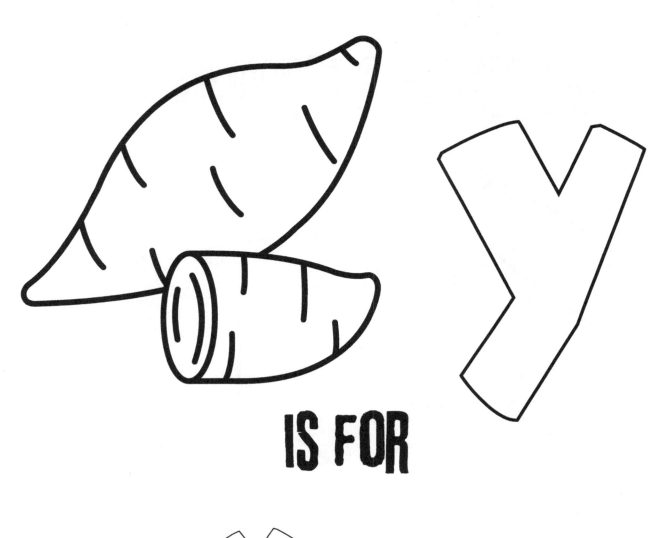

IS FOR

y

I SPY WITH MY LITTLE EYE SOMETHING STARTING WITH

 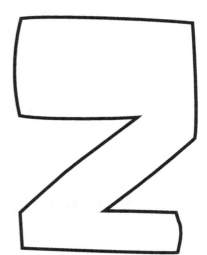

IS FOR

Zucchini

THANK YOU VERY MUCH!

Don't forget to get your FREE Book

SCAN ME

Made in the USA
Middletown, DE
04 December 2022

16892105R00038